# CHIPMUNK COLORING BOOK

CRYSTAL
COLORING BOOKS

Copyright © 2017 Crystal Coloring Books



ISBN-13: 978-1974696246
ISBN-10: 1974696243

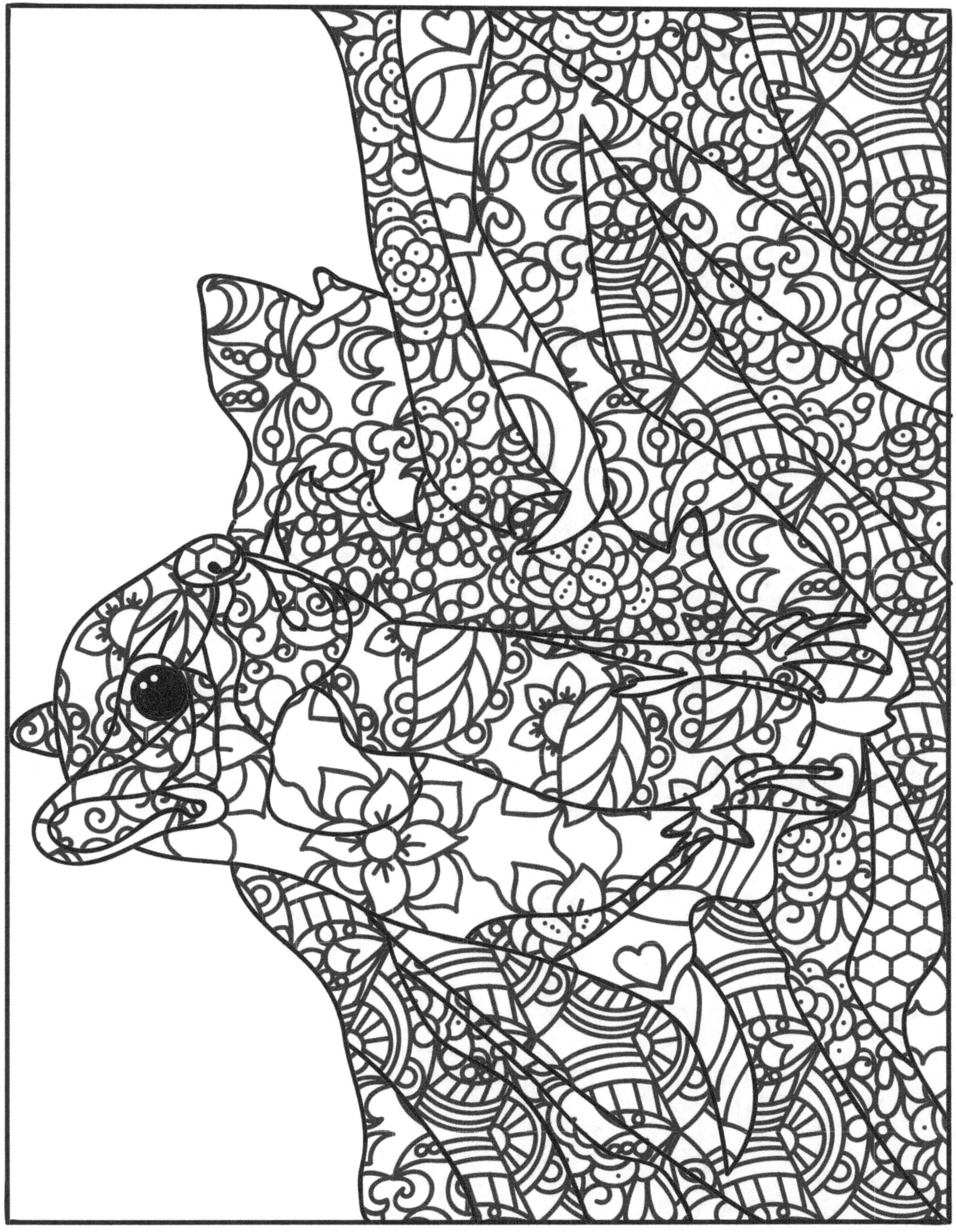

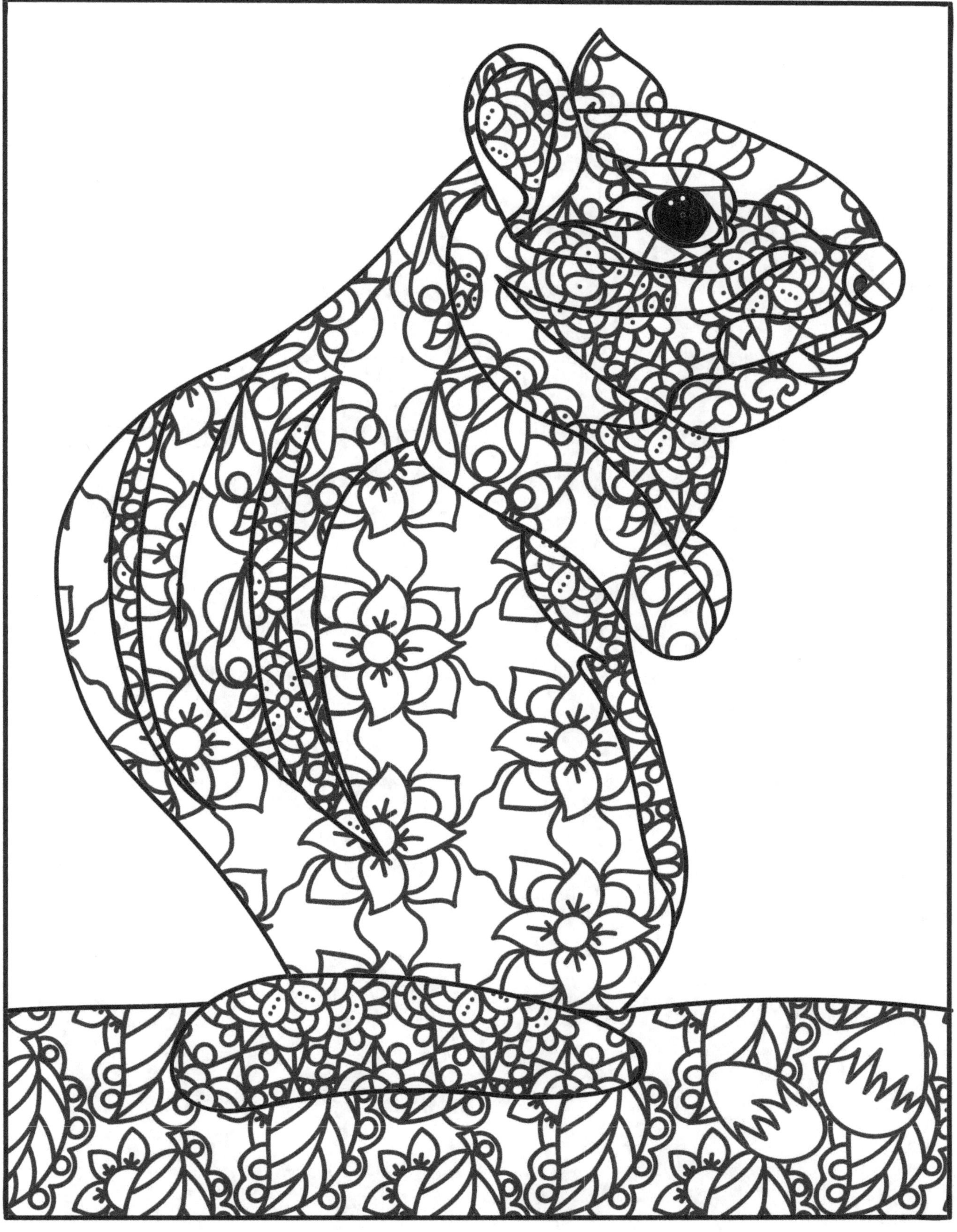

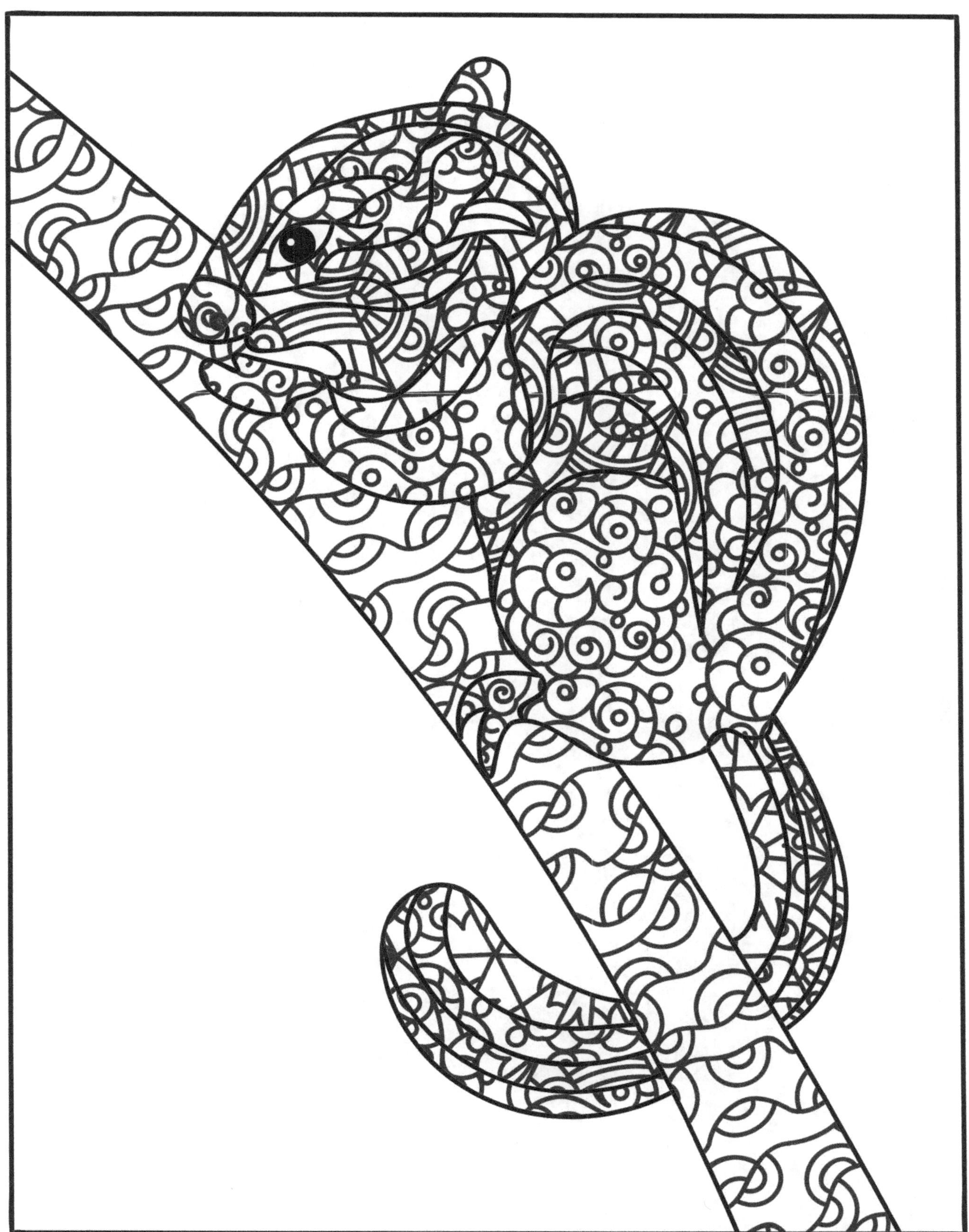

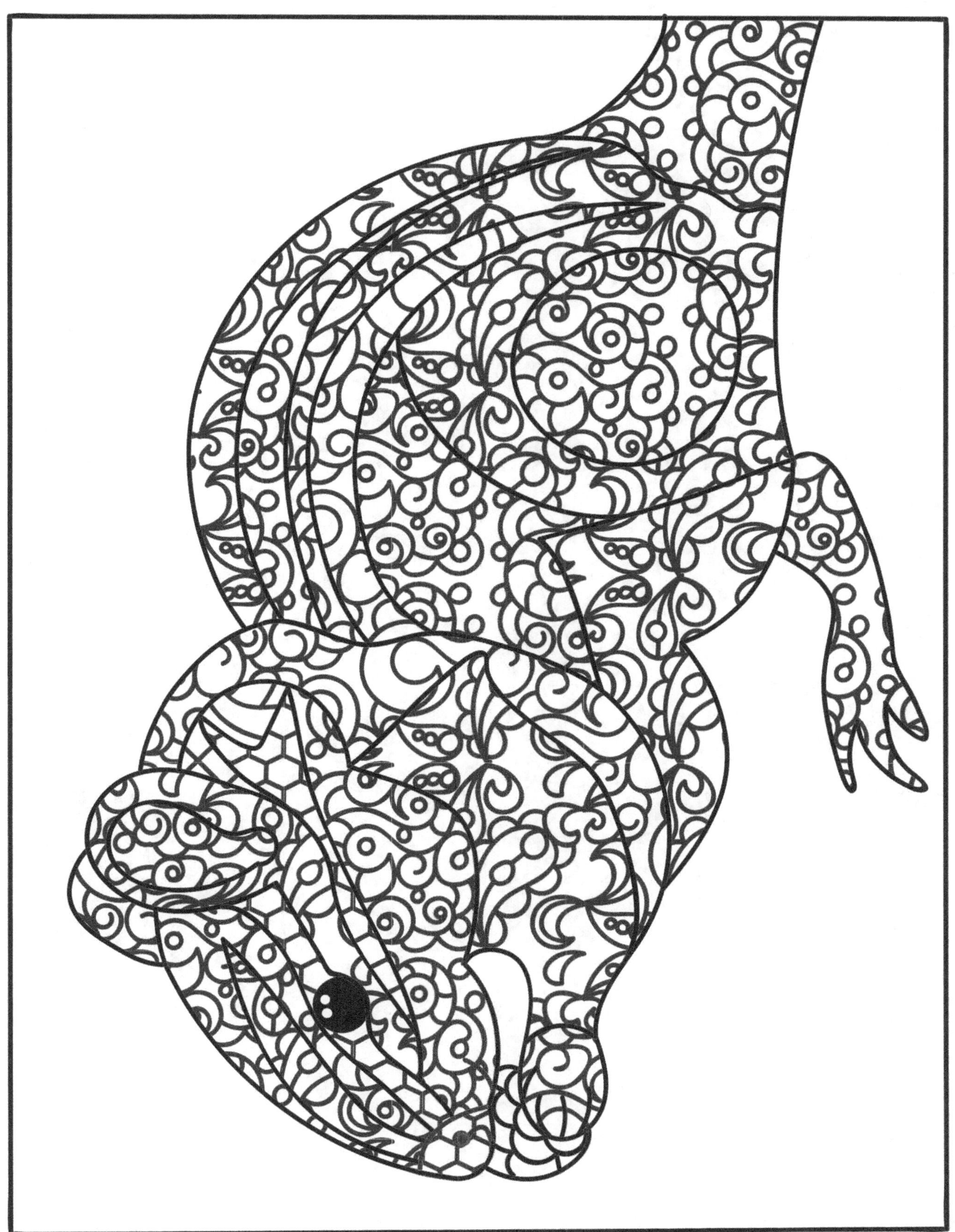

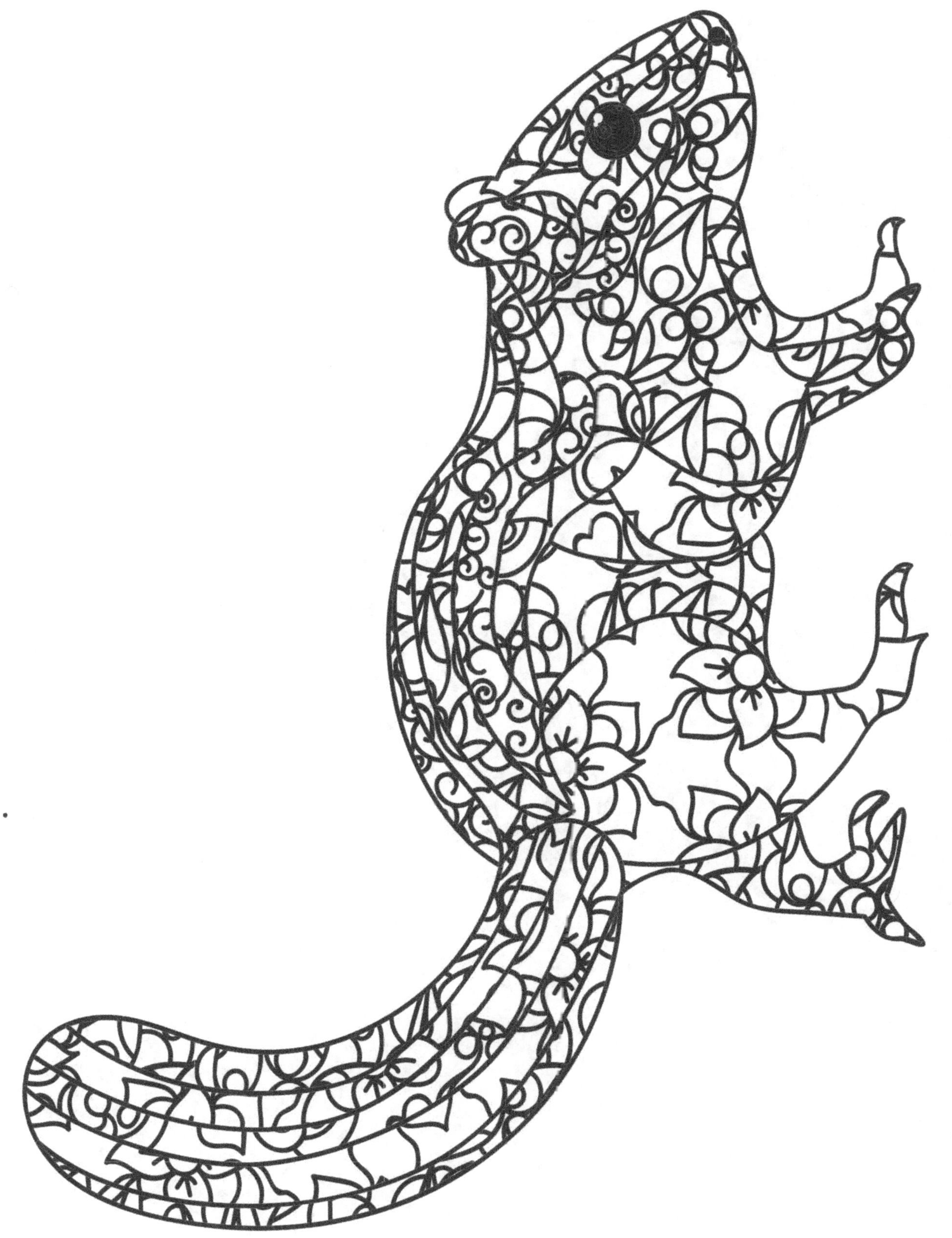

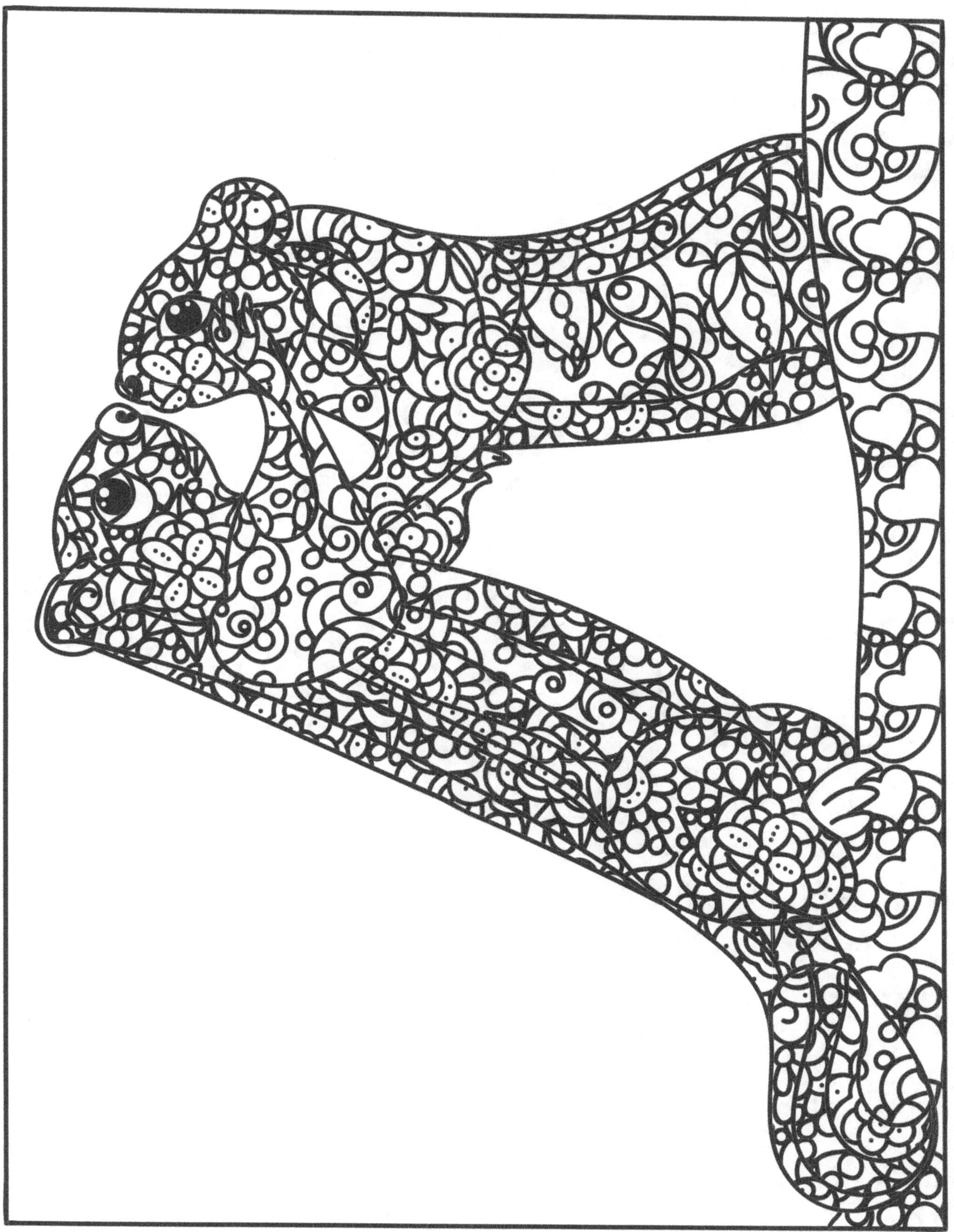

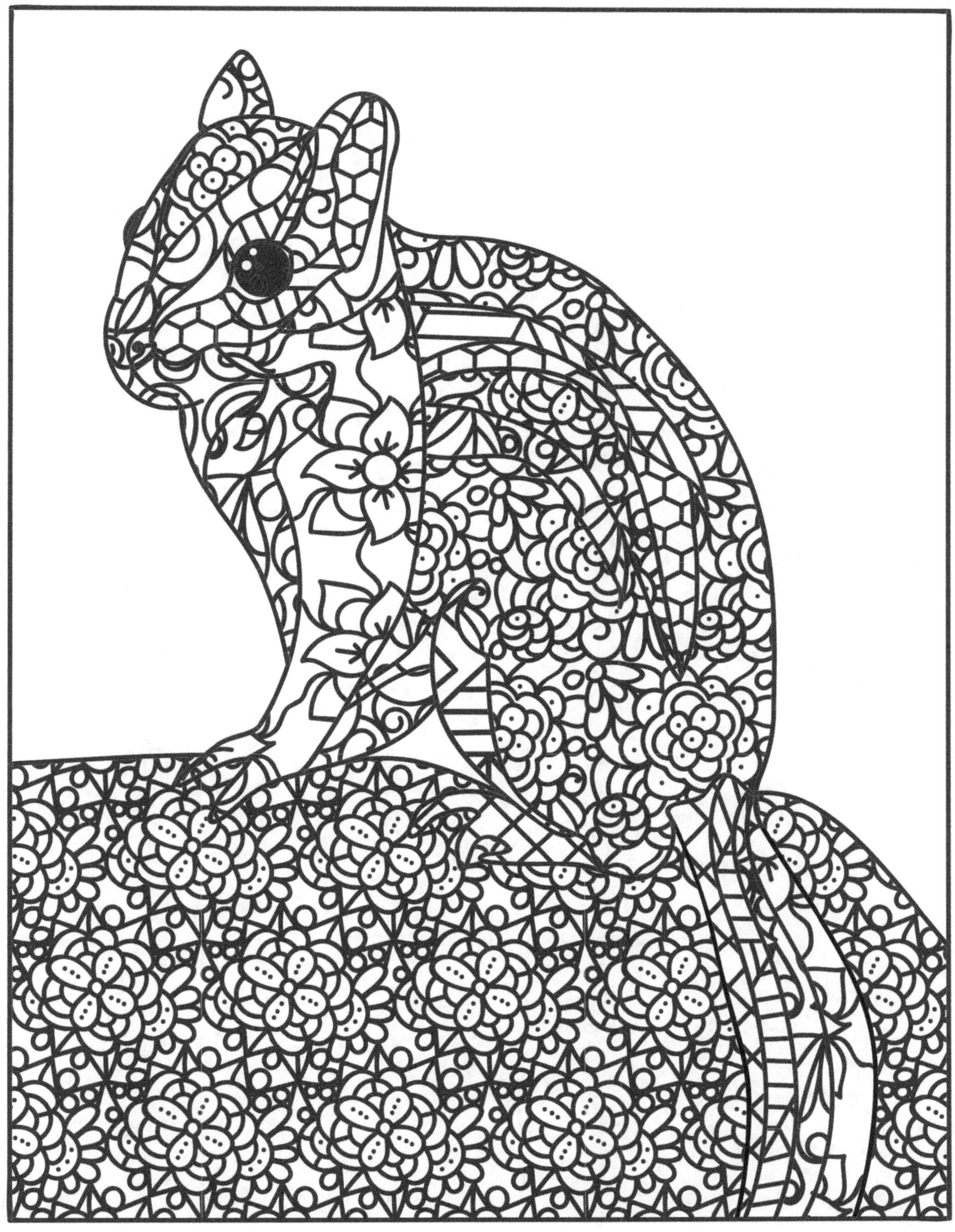

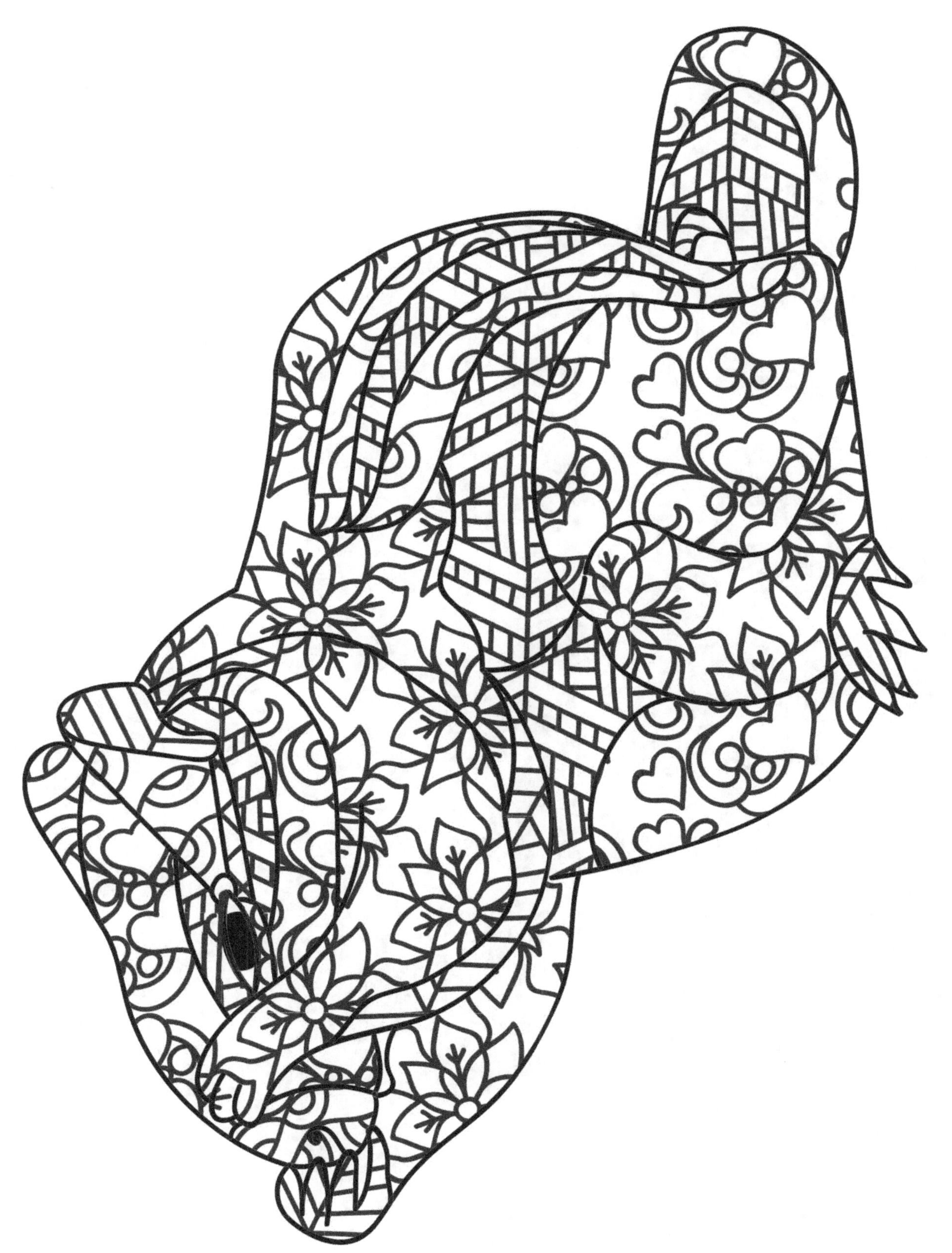

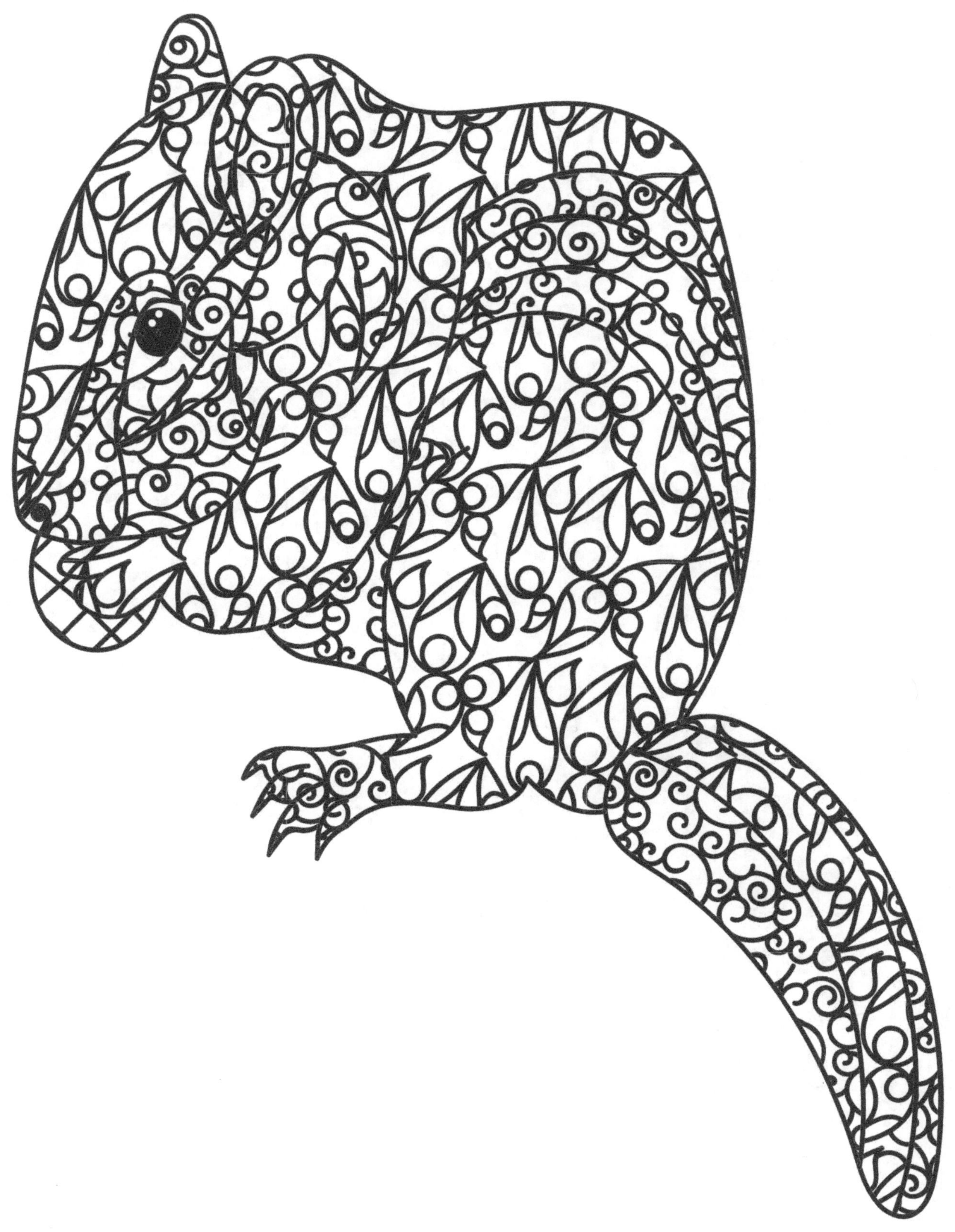

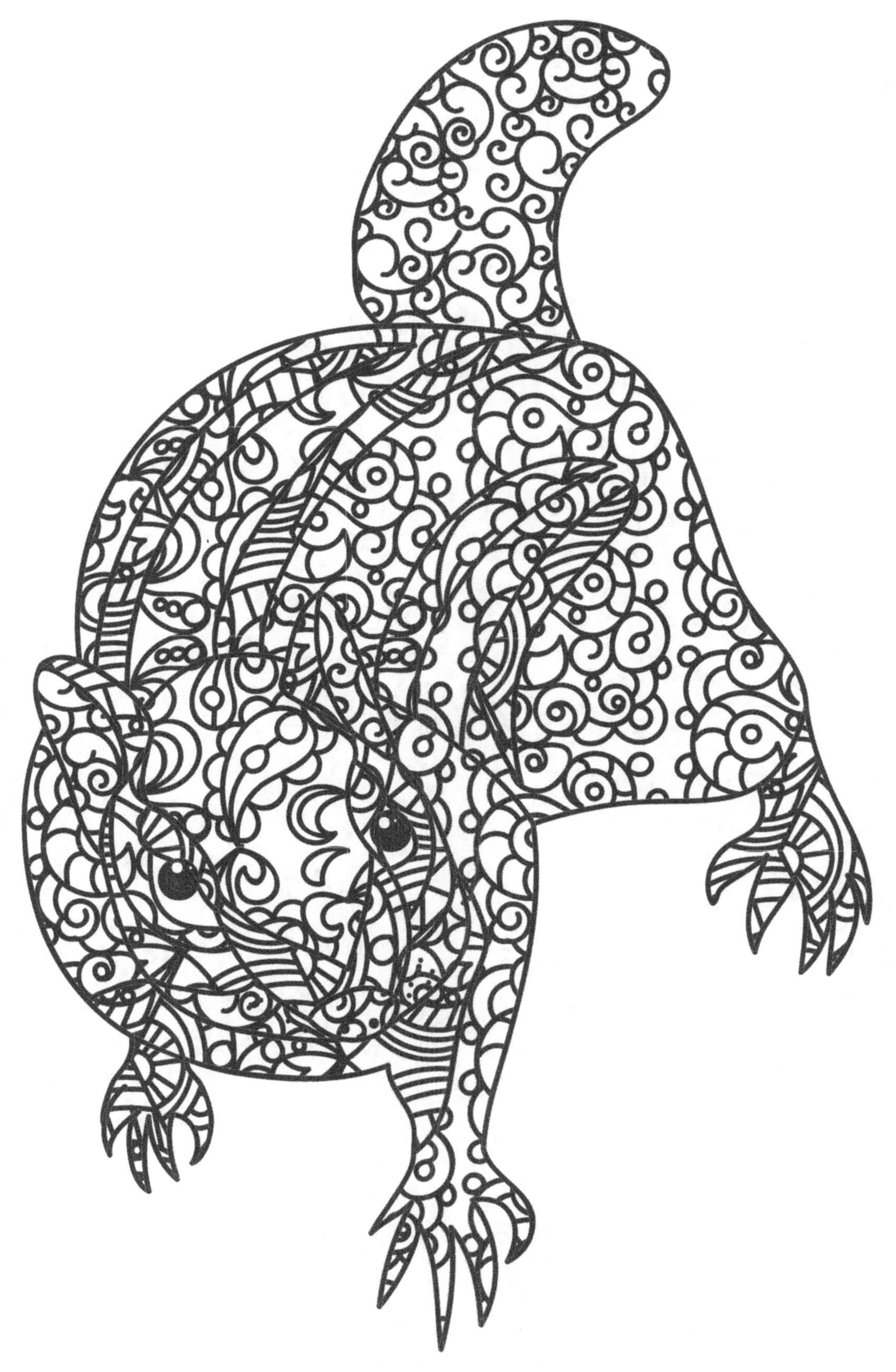

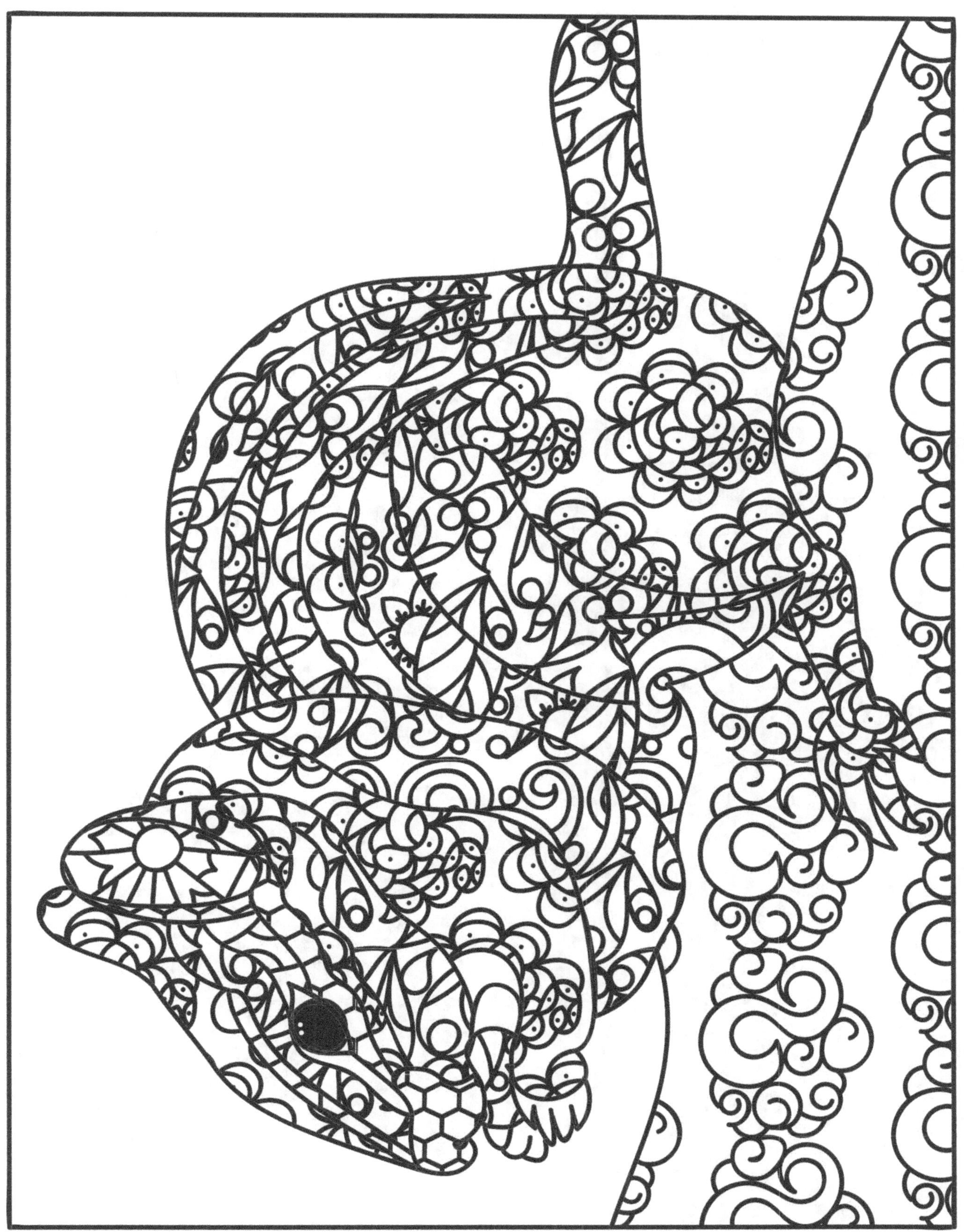

# COLOR TEST PAGE

# COLOR TEST PAGE